THE LIVING ROAD

Milton Moon, A.M., worked in television before studying painting and pottery. His skills as a potter won him a 1994/98 Australian Artists Creative Fellowship. It was on a previous fellowship program in Japan, studying the relationship between Zen Buddhism, Japanese culture and especially the visual arts, that Milton first met the Zen Master whose teachings he shares with the readers of this book.

THE LIVING ROAD

A Meditation Sequence
Milton Moon
(Kako)

MILLENNIUM BOOKS

First published in 1994 by
Millennium Books
an imprint of E.J. Dwyer (Australia) Pty Ltd
3/32-72 Alice Street
Newtown NSW 2042
Australia
Phone: (02) 550-2355
Fax: (02) 519-3218

National Library of Australia
Cataloguing-in-Publication data

Moon, Milton, 1926 –
    The living road.

ISBN 1 86429 008 0.

1. Meditation. 2 Meditations. I. Title.

158.12

Cover design by NB Design
Text design by NB Design
Typeset in 12.5pt by Sun Photoset Pty Ltd, Brisbane
Printed by Australian Print Group, Maryborough, Victoria

10 9 8 7 6 5 4 3 2 1

97 96 95 94

The title *The Living Road* and also the first of the
meditation teachings offered, "The Pure Wind," come from
a verse written by Daito Kokushi (1228–1337), founder of
the Daitoku-ji, Kyoto, Japan. It is said that this verse was
written by him after experiencing profound
enlightenment:

> *"Having once penetrated the cloud barrier*
> *The Living Road opens out*
> *North, East, South and West.*
> *In the Evening, resting,*
> *In the Morning, roaming,*
> *Neither Host nor Guest,*
> *At every step the Pure Wind rises."*

Dedication

To Kobori Nanrei, Abbot of Ryoko-in, Daitoku-ji, Kyoto, Japan, with great respect and gratitude.

He left this life during the writing of this "teaching."

In the tradition of all wise teachers, he taught only that which was needed to those who were in need.

"The warm colored Autumn leaves fade and fall, still the Pure Wind rises."

This teaching is also dedicated to the *hijiri*, the Holy Ones, the sages, the teachers of the market place, whose determined denial of both the prestige and comforts of a monastic life was equalled only by their strength of purpose.

Contents

Foreword 11

Preface 13

Acknowledgments 23

THE PURE WIND

Introduction 27

Day Number Seven (The First Day) 31

Day Number Six 39

Day Number Five 43

Day Number Four 47

Day Number Three 51

Day Number Two 55

Day Number One 59

The Farewell 67

MYSELF, OTHER-SELF, ONESELF

Introduction 73

Meeting the Master 77

The First Day 81

The Second Day 87

The Third Day 93

THE LIVING ROAD

The Fourth Day	99
The Fifth Day	105
The Sixth Day	111
The Seventh Day	115
The Farewell	121

Foreword

ANNE DEVESON

Being with Milton Moon is a satisfying experience, like being with one of his pots. Both the man and his work have a wholeness and an integrity about them. Both reveal surprises—like this book. I had long known that Milton was a student of Zen, I did not know that he had written about it. He told me diffidently. He is a diffident person in many ways, and when finally I saw the manuscript I did so at a time when I was feeling particularly jaded. I was especially leery about books peppered with capital letters and exclamation marks prescribing instant remedies and instant revelations about the meaning of life.

Milton's book is, of course, quite different. It is a quiet book, one that has its own stillness, and one that is simple, wise and refreshing to read. It is the distillation of his experiences in Japan, learning the teachings of Zen and of meditation. He had read deeply and widely on the subject, but that did not impress his Master, who said that instead of just reading about it, one should try to become it.

The first part of this book describes one particular week's meditation course at a Zen Temple in Kyoto. You might say, "But if I read this book, I am still only reading—I am not becoming." What this book does, however, is to take us through that week's experience, so that if we follow and practise the teachings, the reading is the beginning of the becoming.

The second part of the book tries to prompt the questions that will eventually lead to the answers. The two parts flow one into the other. They are practical and explicit. They also stem from an inner one-ness.

Milton first met the Master in 1974, and kept in contact with him until his recent death. The Master took him seriously as a student. At one stage, he told him that he in turn should assume the role of teacher. Yet Milton is a potter, and as such has given us countless works of great strength and beauty. He has not been a teacher of Zen or of meditation. That's what he would say. But through this book he brings the teachings, and through his life and his work, he lives them.

I read the book throughout the night when first I received it, not stopping from the first page to the last, but reading slowly because I felt myself being drawn into an adventure and an experience from which I did not want to escape. And then I read it again, over a one week's period, practising the exercises, as if I too had been present in the Temple. Now I turn back to it when I feel my mind scattered and my self disintegrating. Each time, it reminds me that, almost always, our answers lie within.

Preface

"You will either do it or you won't." It was put to us as directly as that. "You will or you won't."

All of us who studied with the Master found him to be very kind and considerate but direct to the point of luntness. There was no way he could be persuaded to engage in what he thought was idle discussion. "You will or you won't." There was no way one could avoid that sort of statement. He was also quite beyond seeking or needing either our warmth or approval.

The Master seemed to be acutely aware of what was happening in the world beyond his temple but made few concessions to any expectations the twentieth century might have of him. For example, the temple (and garden) under his care were very important: they were a "cultural possession" and their collection of rare art was of such world importance that it ensured a steady stream of eminent people who expected that their interest alone was enough to be granted a "viewing." Most left disappointed. His temple was not open to the public either, although many others nearby made a steady income from the cultural tourist.

The Master was also a "traditionalist" in the way he taught. For instance, he told us *what* to do but did not spend much time in telling us *why* we should do it. Some resented this and never returned. We in our Western world are not only used to explanations—we want them. Without an explanation we have no expectation. But the Master did not feel the need to provide this. After all, we had found our way to his door. Wasn't that in itself reason enough for our being there? His attitude was neither one of reluctance nor disinterest; he knew what he had to do and just did it.

This attitude should have "rubbed off" on me, but apparently there is still much for me to learn because I found difficulty in writing this preface. I know what the Master would have said: "They hold the book in their hands; they will either read it or they won't. Why should they be persuaded?"

Someone I have never met was kind enough to read the unpublished transcript of *The Pure Wind*, the first-written of the teachings, and he had a slightly different view. On first appearances, the scraps offered for his perusal must have looked flimsy and insubstantial and, in his professional judgement, they needed some sort of explanation. The advice he gave, although tempered by caution, was good. He proffered the thought that "readers must be led gently towards practice, attitudes, and finally (hopefully), to a view of the world and themselves that embraces simplicity for its own sake," because "our tradition has developed in other directions." He was right of course when he implied that even though one ought not to try and sell a "message of hope," those to whom the message is being offered could at the very least be given some indication of what to expect. But the Master was also right because *you* at this very moment are holding this small book in your hands and any explanations I give will add nothing to what it already contains. It will either be of some value, or it won't. No one can predict that. Only you will finally know.

The essence of *The Living Road* and its meditation teachings, *The Pure Wind*, and *Myself, Other-Self, Oneself*, has been in existence for many more years than we know, either as insightful philosophy or in a variety of religious forms. Even these pages which you are holding have been written and rewritten over recent years and have been passed from hand to hand. For some the message has lacked importance but for others who had not as yet found any other "Way," it has at least pointed to the path they have been seeking.

There have been some who have clasped it to their hearts because it contained the "something" they wanted and needed at that particular time. A young Japanese girl who was dying of cancer called The Pure Wind "her treasure." She was far from her own land and quite possibly because of that the teaching seemed to possess a special value and drew her closer to a source which others might not yet wish to clasp as eagerly.

Thus, while some people afflicted with illness or world-weariness have used it, there are others yet to use it. There are some doctors, too, who have borrowed it and used it freely.

The message of *The Living Road* comes from the meditative traditions of the East. I became acquainted with it through living in Japan but the tradition itself did not begin there. It had been transplanted from China. Much earlier it had been nurtured in India, and long before that time it had existed in one form or another as part of the ebb and flow of wisdom, perhaps even in places long since forgotten.

Most of our small group who attended the Zen Temple in Kyoto were Westerners. The reason for us choosing that particular temple could have been the working of fate, or more likely it may have been the fact that the Master spoke English and not all of us spoke Japanese, or even if we did, our grasp of the language was not as good as was his of English. The Master was also a scholar and taught comparative theology at a Buddhist university. This meant that if he ever needed to dispute a point he could do so with authority. In any case, for whatever reason, over the years a number of Westerners had rung the bell outside his temple seeking admission. This was not usual because most found their way to the Soto temples, which seemed to possess more of a missionary zeal than was usual for the Rinzai sect.

When I first met the Master I told him that I was undertaking a study of the claimed or actual relationship between Zen Buddhism and Japanese culture. At that time in the West, there was considerable interest in this subject, but there was also much misunderstanding and misuse of what is called Zen. I told the Master of (what I thought to be) the enormity of my reading on the subject but this did not impress him greatly. He suggested that a better way to further my understanding might be from the "inside out" and instead of just reading about it I should try to "become" it. But he also made it clear that any commitment to do this had to be more than casual.

The Master did not seek students, but neither (as far as I knew) did he drive anyone away. Nor did he preach a specialized gospel but merely pointed to the "way" we could take. He also pointed to traditions outside his own as being of equal importance. With him there was no sin of pride. He said quite simply, "You say God, I say Buddha."

Among my companions from the West was an eminent neurologist from an important medical center in America; he was studying neurological and psycho-physiological aspects of Zen meditation. Another who attended was a political scientist who had her own reasons for finding her way there. A Jesuit priest who attended was undertaking a phenomenological survey of Japanese religions. The Japanese who attended came and went, and outside temple times we had very little contact. There were some who did not come as regularly as others and there were also the occasional ones who attended for a few weeks and were not seen again.

Some of us spent a year there, others even more. There were no financial obligations of any kind. We were asked for nothing except our sincerity. However, we did spend some of our time doing the menial tasks necessary for the upkeep of the temple. I enjoyed keeping the very beautiful cemetery clean and weeded. There was always wood to be chopped and some of us were much better at that than others. I think even the Master kept a respectful distance.

We all had our regular confrontations with the Master during the period known as San-zen, when he tested our progress, but none of us discussed this with anyone else and in fact were asked not to. Occasionally we would hear the Master shouting at someone but we could not know why.

I recall one young American who did complain that she was dismissed from the Master's presence almost as soon as she confronted him. I wondered whether this was thought to be a necessary part of her training. She chose not to stay long and that seemed a pity.

It was during this period at the Temple that I came to realize some of the difficulties in teaching meditation. This was of interest to me because at that time I was a teacher of another discipline. Though far removed from what I was learning there, the problems seemed to parallel each other in some ways. My questions to the Master might have revealed something of this for at the end of my time there, somewhat surprisingly, he suggested that on my return home I might begin a small meditation group. I never did this, for several reasons. In any case, he was not to know that in my country such an activity was bound to meet with scepticism and, in all probability, ridicule. I also felt unequal to the task.

Yet for many years I could not rid myself of the sense of obligation to someone who had unquestioningly agreed to instruct me and others like me without expectation of any return. It was at this point I resolved at the very least to attempt to put something on paper.

When I first put these notes together I did not use my own name, not only for personal reasons but because I believed that a name in itself is not important. I took the view that the contents of the teaching merited much more attention than the author's identity. In actual fact, "Kako," the name I used when I first assembled these notes, is a proper name in that it was given to me; it is a "Go," an "Azana," or as we say in the West, a nom de plume. The tradition of using alternative names has long been a custom in Japan. Many artists and writers had a number of such names; they often changed them when they embarked on a new direction in their work. I too preferred this sort of anonymity. But this produced its own dilemma.

Firstly, I am not Japanese and not to use my own name might have been misunderstood. Secondly, "Kako" had in fact become an amalgam of teachers, as I sought to produce an acceptably Western approach to the subject. But the fact that "Kako" was also *me* did have some advantages. Being Western it was to be hoped that I was also better able to understand the expectations of the Western mind and the difficulties the Westerner can encounter in trying to learn a skill which often seems unnecessarily abstract, or worse, irrational. So in the end I decided to use both of my names . . .

These were not the major problems, however. The real challenge was to try to convey the intangible. For example, how does one express in words the subtle message which can lie behind a single word, or a telling glance, or the reason hidden within an abrupt question? Often, the most forceful of the Master's teachings were like that. Also, how can one explain the uncanny insight possessed by a genuine Master and his awareness of the exact moment when the student is most receptive to a particular point? The Master with whom I studied used very few words, quite often too few for the average Westerner, but the ones he did use were both measured and forceful. He also preferred that we find for ourselves not only the answers we were seeking, but also the questions that would prompt those answers.

I sent him the manuscript of *The Pure Wind* seeking both his permission and approval. Instead of writing a diary account of my own learning period, I chose to present the material in a workshop form more suited, I thought, for Western use. Inevitably my own interpretations of his teaching merged with a certain amount of literary invention. Even now as I reread what I have written, I ask myself, "Did I write that or are those the actual words of the Master?" I hoped he would accept my efforts.

The Master wrote back with some suggestions and also some queries but did not demur at any liberty I had taken in giving the work a more palatable form for a Western reader. He may have thought, "They will either read it, or they won't," and left it at that. This of course is true.

Reading it is not the problem: doing it is the difficult part. Each of the teachings contained within *The Living Road* will take one short hour to read, after which the initial practice will take only a week to do, but it will still take a lifetime to perfect—unless of course one is endowed with extreme good fortune.

What is written in the following pages is a simple approach to understanding the technique of meditation. Each of the teachings is in the form of a one-week meditation workshop. The first of them, "The Pure Wind" teaching, is a self-contained beginner's course and claims to be nothing more. On the surface it appears simple to do, yet it is also hard. In Japan, meditation is known to be "hard work." There are other ways from other traditions that claim to be easy, but in reality they also are difficult. The hardest part is in first disciplining our conceit—in "knowing that we do not know."

Restless Westerners often try to both read and master such a teaching in one afternoon, but that is not the way. Ours is very much an "instant" age and patience is a rare attribute. Yet this is what is needed.

Finally, though you will either do it properly or you won't, the choice is yours. But if you do practise it the way it is intended, you may be surprised at what happens.

This then is my preface and my "explanation." The message carried by *The Living Road* is offered in the hope that, even in some small part, it may help discharge my feeling of obligation to someone who seemed to be quite beyond any need for personal reward and who followed his path for reasons apparently beyond any personal commitment or even choice. I know also that my sense of obligation can never really be discharged because it too is beyond personal choice and will last forever.

As I used to say when I was a small child, "for ever and ever ... that really *is* forever."

Acknowledgments

Believing, as I do, that no human creative effort belongs to any one person, I wish to mention some who played a part, even unwittingly, in this work.

Jan Hodge, who at one particular time needed much help, nevertheless played a part as a listener and participant.

Ikuko Sasabuchi took the Pure Wind teaching to her heart and in so doing encouraged the author to follow his own beliefs even further.

Neville Farrall gave perceptive and valuable help with the Pure Wind manuscript.

Charles E. Hulley, whom I have never met, added much burnish and did so with skill and wisdom. He led the author to understand that things of value might be all too easily obscured beneath an overburden of unnecessary or excessive explanation.

Finally, Harold Stewart, poet, scholar, long-time resident of Japan and follower of the Pure Land path, has with great kindness and many letters patiently led the author to see beyond the rigid limitations of his own patterns of thought. With all humility I acknowledge his unintended inspiration.

THE
PURE
WIND

Introduction

The Master was in working clothes. There was always work to be done—vegetables to be tended, rubbish to be collected, firewood to be gathered, the cemetery of many centuries to be weeded and swept. He held up one hand and with the other grasped the tip of a finger, saying, "A fingertip taste is useless. Some do that and think they have learned to meditate. Do not come at all if that is what you want ..."

A small group of us, from several countries, had met at the Temple to take part in what was to be a one-week period of meditation instruction. The Master had asked us to meet the day prior to the commencement of the "workshop." None of us knew who instigated the "workshop" or how each of us happened to be there.

The Master continued ... "It is not necessary that I ask why you wish to meditate. It is not necessary to know how whole or how incomplete you are or if you are hurt and suffer pain, or bear resentment. It is not necessary to know anything about your life until now. There is no end to searching amongst the remnants of the past ... that is like searching in the bottom of a muddy barrel ... There is no end to that.

"But there is another way:
it will not cost you money;
it will not bring you harm.
But do not come if you do not want to do it properly. Not doing it properly might bring you regrets.

"How will you know if you are doing it properly? Keep asking yourself: 'Am I doing it properly?' You will know.

"Nor is it important to know if you have a particular religious commitment. Some say 'God,' others say 'Buddha' or worship other Holy Ones. Some people these days do not follow any particular religion but pray in their own way. Others would like to pray but do not know *how* or *what* to pray.

"Some religions put great store in observing strict moral codes, whilst others are less strict. *Faith* is central to most religions ... and prayer. In Buddhism there are also many differences in practice. In the Dhyana sects of Buddhism, meditation is most important.

"Meditation is not prayer, it is something else. We meditate so that we might become free of illusions. Illusions are self-created, but when you reach the final stage of meditation you could not be deluded even if you wanted to be.

"Forget such terms as 'enlightenment' or 'satori' and do not search for them. Do not feel pride in any self-development you think you have made. Do not try to understand too much about meditation, and please do not ask me for explanations because I am not sure I can give them to you.

In a Zen Temple there is a prescribed pattern to daily living, with work to be done, sutras to be recited, meditation to be practised ... often for long periods. But all of you here today live ordinary lives, everyday lives, and you will have to regulate your own practice and impose your own disciplines. It is no different to running a race: you have to train your whole body to face the strains that it will cause.

Remember always, we are both Mind and Body. Each is separate, yet they belong together. So we must train both, and that is why we are here today.

"We have seven days together and in that short space of time I shall teach you how to meditate. Seven days is a short time, yet it might seem like an eternity before it is over. Now please go and we shall meet again tomorrow to begin our training in earnest."

Day Number Seven

(THE FIRST DAY)

On the first morning the Master met us in a small room adjacent to the entrance-room of the Temple. We had left our shoes on the verandah step leading into the Temple. We had been instructed to leave them neatly, in the pre-scribed manner—placed parallel with the toes pointing outwards. We were to find that even this simple task was taken with some seriousness. "Your shoes too are your Mind," we were told. "Do not leave them scattered around in an undisciplined way. Remember, everything you do is a reflection of your Mind."

The Master entered the room but did not formally greet us. He began . . .

"You can only meditate when you have prepared your Mind properly. When a carpenter gets ready for work he first prepares his tools. A musician tunes the instrument to be played and a painter prepares brushes and paper, or canvas. We too have to prepare . . . but the tools we use are our minds. We have to learn to empty our minds so that the jumble of thoughts that usually follow one on top of the other do not intrude.

"It is not easy to discipline our minds... we are victims of thoughts. Our minds are unruly... and to tame our minds is not easy and most people give up too quickly.

"Now let us begin. This is our first day, but this week we shall work backwards. Today is the seventh day... tomorrow will be the sixth, the next day the fifth, and so on until we reach Day Number One.

"Shortly you will be taken to the Meditation Hall. You will be shown where to sit, after which you can practise some of the things I will tell you to do. As you are beginners you will not be expected to undertake long periods of 'sitting,' but during this week here, and also when you return to your homes, you should practise as often as you can, even for short periods, until meditation becomes second-nature.

"You should also practise alone as much as possible. Later it will not matter so much—you will be surprised at how well you can practise, even in a busy street. In the beginning though, distractions will be a hindrance so do try and be alone.

"Also, this week, when you leave the Temple, do not spend too much time talking, especially about what you are beginning to experience. Remember, time is precious. Life in the busy world does not leave us much time so do not waste your spare moments. You must develop good habits and one of these is learning to snatch every available moment to go deep into your minds.

"In the Meditation Hall we sit in the prescribed manner. This is good for discipline and also we do not distract or disturb others who are 'sitting.' In your own homes though, at this stage, it does not matter how you 'sit.' It will be better though if you are still. It is not important whether you are sitting on a chair or on a bed, or even half-sitting on the kitchen table, but you must be still. Try to visualize stillness within you and all about you.

"The next thing you must practise is *relaxed awareness.* To do this you can begin by opening and closing your eyes, very slowly. Next, move your shoulders up and down, but again do this very slowly. Lift your shoulders up and then let them drop, and then relax your arms and hands. Gently open and close your hands... you will begin to feel them become heavy. You can spend a little time practising this sort of relaxing as it is most important. One might get the impression that Zen monks in a temple are sitting very straight and are therefore strained, but this is not so; they are very relaxed, but they are also wide awake and alert.

"On this first day you must not confuse yourselves by having too many things on which to concentrate. Learning to relax is extremely important, then once you have begun to feel relaxed in your body you can begin to work on your mind. We must learn to tame our minds and to do this, I want you to first practise *slow-motion soft-focusing.* In the Meditation Hall there is not much for you to focus on, but in your own homes this exercise will be much easier.

"At first I do not want you to focus on things close to you, but on something preferably a little distance away—perhaps the other side of the room in which you sit. This could be a vase of flowers, a cup and saucer... it might even be a picture on a wall. It doesn't matter what you look at, just so long as you have one thing on which to concentrate. This is very important, so don't take this exercise too lightly, or skip over it too quickly.

"Look at the object you have chosen. Look above it. Look behind it, or below it. Do *not* squint your eyes to see it more clearly, but just look at it as if you were doing it in *slow-motion.*

"Perhaps I should explain this more carefully. Not many of us give anything our full attention. We lead busy lives and our eyes and our attention dart all over the place. We have learned to switch our attention *on* and *off* with lightning speed. But now we must learn to slow down our mind-processes and train ourselves to give things our full attention. You may think you are doing this, but mostly you are *not*, and you *will never meditate properly* until you have learned to slow your Minds down and to hold your attention for quite long periods. This is what we will begin to learn today.

"Look at the object you have chosen. Move your eyelids up and down, very, very slowly, and then, without squinting or straining, *let* the object you are looking at come into focus. Clear your Minds of everything else, other than *slow-motion soft-focusing*.

"This next part of our training is also important. I want you to realize *when* the object is fully focused, and *when* it goes *out* of focus. You will notice that once you have the object clearly imprinted in your brain, it will begin to go out of focus. It is almost as though you are saying that you no longer need to fully focus on the object as you *know* what it is. You must learn to recognize when you *are* focused and when you are *not* focused. You must learn the difference between giving something the full presence of your Minds and *when* you are losing attention. In meditation this is of the utmost importance, especially when you are in the learning stages.

"So the first thing I want you to do is to train your focusing. Relax your bodies then softly and slowly focus on the object you have chosen. See *how slowly* this can be done. Do this many times until you feel you are beginning to do it properly.

"The next thing I want you to do is to relax your focus and then very slowly bring your attention back to yourself. I want you to half-close your eyes and think about your face and head.

"Our faces are full of muscles. We can move our mouths, stretch or wrinkle the muscles on our foreheads, and move our ears. I want you to relax your forehead and your nose and ears and then bring your attention to your lips. Close them tightly, then relax them. Do this several times, after which I want you to imagine you are saying the word 'seven.' I want you to say it to yourself, over and over again.

"Today is Day Number Seven, as I have already told you, and all day long I want you to say the word 'seven.' You will not be saying the word with your mouth and vocal cords, but it might be easier for you to move your lips as you silently say the word. Breathe out and say 'seven.' Breathe in and 'seven' will come back in. But *do not make a sound.* Say it slowly, *in slow-motion:* S-E-V-E-N. Breathe out and then draw your breath back in and let 'seven' follow your breath.

"These exercises can be done everywhere—in the tram or bus—anywhere at all. There is always something to focus your eyes on, and you can also practise saying 'seven' to yourself. You don't have to move your lips of course. But you *must do this exercise properly.* Remember, your minds are very clever. They are used to doing many things at once, and doing them all at lightning speed, but this week we are learning to slow down our minds.

"Once you have mastered these two exercises I have a game for you to play. I now want you to say the 'seven' which you have been breathing in and out, not with your lips, but in your head. But I don't want you to have the sound just anywhere inside your head—I want you to locate it wherever you want it to be. I want you to imagine the sound can be behind your forehead, or at the back of your head, or close to your left temple, or left ear, or your right temple, or right ear. After a while you will notice that the 'sound' of 'seven' can be anywhere you want it to be. Wherever you place your 'presence of mind' the sound can be there too. But to do this properly you must first learn to relax totally.

"Relax your eyes, then open and close them as slowly as you can. Relax your jaw muscles, but keep your mouth closed except for the times you are saying 'seven' with your lips. Remember you can make the 'sound' of 'seven' be where you want it to be—*it is all in your mind*. Of course it is easy to imagine 'seven' coming from your mouth— sounds always come from your mouth—but I want you to practise putting the 'sound' where you want it to be. If you want it to be near your left ear, or right ear, incline your head to the side you want. With a little practice you will be surprised how well you can do it. But do not be anxious or tense whilst you do this: it is a game, but at the same time it is *not* a game. What we are doing is nothing more than learning to train both our other-awareness and our self-awareness. The greatest hindrance to meditation is 'intrusive thoughts' and you will find that these occur in endless succession until you learn to train your minds.

"This week you will learn a lot about meditation, but you will learn more quickly if you do what I ask of you, without questioning. It will be a mistake if you look for reasons, or mentally argue with what I ask you to do. Even if you can't see the importance of them, please take these exercises seriously—they are not as easy as they might appear to be. What else must you do? Just keep asking yourself whether you are *doing it properly*.

"You will now be taken to the Meditation Hall and I shall see you tomorrow."

Day Number Six

The morning of the Second Day we met at the Temple, as we had done the previous day. Before going to the Meditation Hall the Master addressed us:

"Yesterday I gave you some exercises which will be of benefit to you for the rest of your lives. The object of these exercises is not for you to learn tricks that you can perform like a monkey, but at the same time, they can be used as a device to help you when you need them. For instance, the slow-motion soft-focusing technique can be of enormous benefit when you are nervous, or suffering stress. We all become nervous at times but once you acknowledge this, the effect can be lessened simply by shifting your attention onto something and focusing on it, using the slow-motion technique. The more you practise this, the quicker and better the results will be. In this way, the technique is also a therapy.

"At the same time it is a quick technique for entering a meditation state. A lot of people waste time unnecessarily trying to meditate properly. Meditation is not a struggle. It is a relinquishing of what I call 'a too-active ego state.' But more of this later.

"You should also practise total relaxation, total submission, but this takes time to learn. I often tell students that this lesson can be learned better if you do it a hundred times a day. That sounds like a lot of time, but it need not be. All you need to do is ask yourself how relaxed can you become in one minute, or half a minute, or in ten seconds. Does this sound impossible? It won't be by the end of this week. By this, I do not mean the sort of relaxation you might experience when you lie down on a comfortable bed. You must practise relaxation in every possible posture—when sitting, standing, or even when you are uncomfortable. In fact, you must practise relaxation when you *are* uncomfortable. Also, you must learn to sit straight, but we shall go more into this later.

"Today I want you to do a few more things. Yesterday you focused on something a distance from you. For the rest of this week, each day I want you to bring the object closer to you, until it is very close, but please do this in stages. Do not try and hurry our lessons.

"I want you to do slow-motion soft-focusing hundreds of times each day, until it becomes a habit. You must become aware of when things are *in* focus and when they are *not*. Also practise *opening* and *closing* your eyes slowly, but each time you do it, try to do it even more slowly.

"Yesterday I asked you to say the word 'seven.' Today you will say the word 'six.' Yesterday though, I asked you to try and locate where the sound of 'seven' was inside your head. You will remember that the word was not said aloud, but was only in your mind. Nonetheless it is still possible to shift the sound from place to place. This is easier for some of you than it is for others.

"Today, I want you to say the word 'six,' in your mind only, but I want you to imagine you are saying it very loudly, almost as though you were calling out to someone. Then I want you to call it out less loudly, then lesser still, and lesser, and finally make it a soft whisper. Do this again and again, all day long. Driving a car, travelling on public transport, walking along the street, keep saying 'six.' At first *loud*, then *softer*, and softer, and softer, until it is just a whisper in your mind, one that you can scarcely hear... so softly in fact that you can't be sure you have said it at all.

"This is not such a difficult exercise and for some of you it might be easier than the one we did yesterday. It is all in your mind of course and not very different from imagining that we are talking to someone. So today, I want you to say 'six' again and again. If it helps, coordinate the word with your outgoing breath, and if this is still difficult, move your lips as though you were whispering the word to someone. But start loudly, then turn down your 'mind-volume' until you can scarcely hear yourself. It is not too different from calling out 'help' or 'hooray' in your mind.

"Finally, remember, when you have learned to meditate, you do not need a special place. In fact, you must learn to take your meditation with you wherever you are. Meditation must become part of your daily life, all the time.

"Do not waste your time... do your exercises... do not ask questions... do not look for answers because they will come of their own. Keep asking yourself: 'Am I doing it properly?' Do not try and understand, intellectually, what we are doing here. In fact, tell yourself, as I was told to tell myself: 'Know that you do not know.'

"You are already beginning to train yourself for the real business of meditation. Don't waste your time ... keep asking yourself: 'Am I doing it properly?'

"Now please go to your tasks and we shall meet again tomorrow morning."

Day Number Five

The Master said:

"Counting today, we have five days left to learn many things. But what we learn is a little different from accumulating a lot of facts and figures to help you pass an examination. What you learn here can't be examined by anyone else. *You* have to sit for your own test, and *you* must award yourself marks. It is not possible to assess your progress by what you have become but rather, by what you have ceased to be. It is only by noticing the growing absence of the less desirable aspects of ourselves that we measure progress. But it is better if we do not measure ourselves at all.

"Once again we begin with our focusing exercises. You are lucky to have eyes with which to see. A blind person cannot focus the way you are able to although, of course, a blind person can focus in other ways. One can focus on a nose, a toe, or the stomach. The stomach is a very good place on which to focus. One can relax one's stomach to such a degree it can almost fall on the floor. Also, if you touch the fingers of one hand with those of the other hand you can notice an amazing range of difference in pressure.

In the same way, a profoundly deaf person can develop controlled awareness. One can concentrate on feelings, or emotions, in the same way an actor might train his or her feelings.

"But you are not blind, or deaf. I merely point out that there are many training devices.

"I will repeat what I want you to do. Make sure you are relaxed. Your shoulders and arms, and your hands and fingers should be relaxed. You will notice that your arms and hands can feel very heavy. Most importantly, let your belly expand. As you breathe in and out, concentrate on the outward breath and let your abdomen and then your belly expand. Don't *make* it expand, *let* it expand. Also, relax your forehead muscles and let your eyelids become a little heavy. Practise opening and closing them in *slow-motion*. When you have done that, do your focusing exercises, but on something a little closer to you. You may by now realize that I am purposely bringing your focusing to where it is all happening—*in your mind*.

"Although you should be relaxed in your body, I now want you to concentrate a little on keeping your backbone as straight as you can make it. Let it be the only stiff part of your body. You will do this easily if you try to sit one inch taller than you are. Also, *do not move*. Remember the saying: 'Sit, but do not wobble.'

"The next thing you must do is say 'five'—not with your mouth and vocal cords, but in your mind. The 'five' can be said in many different ways. Yesterday you practised saying 'six' loudly, then less loudly, and so on, until it was so softly said it was scarcely there at all. Today though, I want you to say 'five' in every conceivable way. I want you say it in a tone that suggests *surprise*, then say it *peacefully*, then *softly*, as though to a sleeping child. Then say 'five' with *anger*, and most importantly, with *gentleness*. After all that, try and say the word without any overtones at all—that is not so easy. Then, finally, say it with lessening amounts of emphasis until it disappears. But, do everything with a feeling of *relaxed awareness*.

"When you leave here today, I want you to ask yourself the question—ask it over and over—'why do I want to learn to meditate?' Ask yourself that question, but do *not* supply the answer. *If* and *when* the answer does come, it will come of itself.

"I want you to do all these things today. It has not taken me very long to tell you what to do, but it will take you all day long to do it properly.

"Now please go to your meditation, asking yourself, 'Am I doing it properly?' I shall see you tomorrow."

Day
Number
Four

The Master said:

"You are at the halfway mark. Today is Day Four, with only three more to go. I asked you to ask yourself why you wanted to learn Meditation. It is a serious question and I want you to keep it in your mind all the time. But if you find yourself manufacturing an answer, take no notice, because any answer you 'make up' will be far short of the mark. The real answer will come to you sometime, and when it does it will come quite suddenly, catching you by surprise. You will then realize just how inadequate any answer you might have invented would be.

"It was said by a sage that it takes only a 'fraction of an inch and Heaven and Earth are miles apart.' Not many people meditate properly. Most often there is that 'fraction of an inch' that separates them from full participation, or full absorption. As I have told you, meditation is not something which you can learn, after which you sit for an examination to see how many points you will be awarded. An experienced Master can measure a student's progress, but in most cases a Master is not available. This is not necessarily bad, because within all meditative traditions thousands have not had Masters. I might be able to guide you in your efforts but it is *you* doing the work. It is you who has to experience what is meant by the 'fraction of an inch' that separates Heaven from Earth.

"Please do not think I am making light of your efforts if I liken them to learning to ride a bike. At first you will wobble all over the place but then, when you ride better, you won't need anyone to tell you—*you* will know. But you must always beware of self-deception. Just keep asking yourself: 'Am I doing it properly?'

"It is good to have some self-doubt. It is wise to mistrust yourself a little. We are all prone to cutting corners and we can all be caught up in the myriad images of the wandering mind. The Mind is a marvellous playground. A stray thought, an alluring vision, and we might as well be a million miles away. The choice *is* yours ... all you have to do is train your mind. The brain in your head is a marvellous implement, but it is your Mind that directs and uses it.

"Use your Mind and train your brain. Your brain has to perform a multiplicity of functions, many at the one time. Think of the times one would use it when driving a car. It has to register traffic lights, pedestrians and a million other things. You can also train your brain to be a sort of watchdog, to keep an eye on yourself.

"Your mind-brain-body, working in unison, can do many things at the one time. You can listen to and appreciate music, and look at art at the same time. You can read a book or carry on a conversation yet still be aware of many things that are happening elsewhere. It is true that each of these things does not receive the benefit of a fully focused attention, but this does not seem to matter. Anyway, our lives are too full to give everything our full attention. But you *cannot* do this when you meditate. The true benefits of meditation only occur when it *is* the centre of concentrated attention. Even that statement is short of the mark .... but we will go into this, more deeply, later.

"Today, once again, do your slow-motion soft-focusing but take another step closer to yourself. If you are doing this properly, what you focus on will *not* appear sharp and hard, but instead it will have a *softness* about it. This will only be apparent if you relax your eye muscles. First you must focus, then allow your focused gaze to become soft. This may take a little time to master, but you will be able to do it. As I have told you, what you are doing is not *making* the focus soft, rather, you are *allowing* it to happen. See if you can practise this. Relax your vision ... do not stare hard ... focus slowly and softly.

"This is our Fourth Day. You must say 'four,' 'four,' 'four,' softly, over and over again. Today though, I want you to feel 'four' everywhere ... in your legs, arms, everywhere. Walking along the street, as you put your foot to the ground, feel 'four' in your very footstep. As you sit in a chair, 'four' sits with you. As you breathe in, 'four' fills your lungs.

"Finally, I must tell you, that in spite of all your good intentions—and this happens also with experienced meditators—there always seems to be some background intrusion that interrupts us. In fact, such intrusions can become a serious impediment. Tomorrow we shall talk about this. Now go and do your work."

Day Number Three

The Master wasted no time with greetings:

"It is a curious human conceit that belittles any effort that can't be measured in terms of percentage, or explained in words. Anyway, the usual way we do these is often inaccurate, or falls far short of real measurement. I have told you to ask yourself: 'Am I doing it properly?' Are you?

"There is a danger point that is reached in any meditation practice. Because you are venturing into a territory that is not your usual abode, it is easy to delude yourself into thinking that something is being achieved. Of course it is natural that you would notice some signs of a growing sincerity and peacefulness—perhaps even a diminishing of excitability or anxiety—but this is not enough. The danger is that you think any such change is *real* achievement: you surround yourself with a cocoon of self-satisfaction and contentment that there has been some measurable change. The wise teachers warned against that by telling their students to raise the feeling of doubt. It is this feeling of doubt that will assist against self-delusion.

"Remember too that there is always the danger of losing your way, or finding something else much more interesting to think about.

"Yesterday, I told you there is a technique for you to use to overcome these 'mind intrusions.' It is very simple really: just keep in mind the image of a busy street, with thousands of people passing by. You do not bump into people; you merely step to one side and move on. Do the same with your busy mind. When thoughts intrude, just move aside and pass on. Do not engage them in conversation—there's no end to that. Excuse yourself, and pass on.

"Again today, do your slow-motion soft-focusing. You should by now be beginning to notice that each object you focus on—if are doing it properly—is beginning to *look* a little different. With proper focusing, things appear *softer*, not *hard-edged* as is usually the case. One is more aware of the *dimension* of an object. If you have found this to be so, you are beginning to see things *as they are*, not as you *think* they are. Remember, you might think these exercises are easy, but they are *not* so. The hardest thing to overcome is conceit, thinking that what you are being asked to do can be easily mastered. It is no different to planting something in a garden: no matter how much you *want* something to grow faster, it *can't* grow any quicker than is normal and natural. *Meditation takes time: it grows as it must, fast or slow.*

"Today I have another so-called 'easy' task for you. Do you remember when you were children, playing games of paper cut-outs? One could invent scenes and give them the illusion of being three-dimensional by cutting-out people, trees, houses and cars. Many of the people we meet in daily life are paper cut-outs... they lack real dimension.

"Today, when you say 'three,' let the word and the thought not just stay in your head, but let it fill your whole body. Feel yourself expanding to the limits of your skin. This is Day Number Three, so let 'three' fill up every corner. A good way of testing this is to look at your hand. Hold it in front of you, palm up ... then focus on it very slowly. Soon it should begin to feel warm. Let it become very relaxed. It may even begin to curl closed as well. If you are relaxing properly you can feel 'three' even reach the very tips of your fingers. When you can learn to do this properly, you will stop being a paper cut-out. Most of the time most of us *are* flat, lacking fullness. It takes a little bit of practice to become *fully* human.

"That is all you have to do today. Please do *not* question what you are doing—just *do it* and let it grow naturally. Nothing can be learned without patience."

Day
Number
Two

The Master said:

"Once there was a painter who was continually being asked about his paintings. His reply was always the same: he said he could not explain them and, in fact, he did not really want to know too much about them. He said that if he examined his every motive the paintings would lose their creative spontaneity and would become self-conscious. He preferred them to grow without being forced. Meditation is like that: if you either try to force it, or seek constant explanations, that essential ingredient, naturalness, will be lost.

"Also, a warning: It is possible, in the protective privacy of your meditation place, to imagine that you are achieving results, but once you are again in the real world you may find that your carefully developed attainments lose their substance and you are again a victim of those things over which you have no control. This is a little like the beautifully nurtured hothouse plant, that looks exquisitely beautiful in a protected environment but which is unable to withstand a sudden transplanting into the real world.

"This is why I put such importance on your living your meditation practice, even as you live your ordinary everyday life. You must learn to steal brief moments, and go deep inside yourself, even as you sit at your desk, or walk the streets. You must also beware of becoming bored. You must learn to go beyond boredom. I will explain this a little more.

"Some years ago there was a scientific evaluation undertaken to try and measure some of the effects of meditation on Zen monks. A group of these monks were connected to machines that measured changes in their brain states whilst they were doing their 'sitting.' Other groups of people (not monks) were similarly measured so that the encephalographic charts could be compared. After the 'sitting' began, they were each 'interrupted' in different ways, with various things such as flashing lights, or sounds, all of which were recorded by the machines.

"In the case of the experienced monks, or other experienced meditators, the sudden changes in the recorded brain patterns were immediately followed by a return to the brain state that existed before the interruption. There were of course differences, depending on their experience. But in the case of the inexperienced meditators, including those who were just sitting quietly, there was an initial response to the interruptions, but then they ceased to respond at all. It was as if there was no interruption at all. What had happened was that they had 'habituated.' They ceased to respond. In common language, they had 'turned off.'

"But the experienced Zen monks remained 'creatively attentive' at all times. They remained in what I call a 'creatively responsive' state. This is quite different from either sleepiness or deep and peaceful repose.

"As for today, again focus on something, but this time very close to you. Open and close your eyes in slow-motion, then softly focus, then allow the object to go out of focus. That is all you need do: *in* focus, *out* of focus.

"Next, breathe in slowly and imagine your body is a hollow column and, as the breath enters you, it fills every corner of the space. Say 'two' with the incoming breath and let it sink down, slowly and even more slowly. Your chest is hollow, as are your abdomen and belly. Let the breath sink into your legs. As you walk, feel 'two' even filling up your feet. You already know you can put your thoughts anywhere you want.

"Another thing, it is often the case that you suddenly become aware of faraway noises, like the rumbling of distant traffic, or the noise of conversation. Ignore them: it is only that you are ceasing to habituate to noises, as you used to do. Let 'two' be your companion today. 'Two' is 'within you and all about you.' Become 'two.'

"Tomorrow is our last day. Please practise properly."

Day Number One

The Master greeted us, asking that we remain after the day's 'session' as he wished to see each of us privately:

"Today is our last day of instruction and tomorrow we shall meet for our last farewells. Up until this morning I have purposely kept my instruction to a minimum. If one is sincere, excessive words are of little value and in fact they often prove a hindrance.

"But today I shall talk a little longer and shall try to think of points I may have neglected to mention. Not that this really matters, because if you are honest in your efforts, the answers you are seeking will appear, as though out of thin air.

"Anyway, I have told you not to seek answers, as your very seeking may be an obstacle. The saying 'when the student is ready the teacher appears' is quite true, but you may be surprised to find that the best teachers do not always come in human form. Sometimes your teacher is a book, or a stray word, but also you may be surprised to find that the teacher is within *you*, and has been there all the time, but you have not been listening. Inner focusing will awaken you to the 'teacher within.'

"I have asked you to practise focusing... not only with your eyes, but also with your ears—in fact with your whole being. I want you to practise not only until it becomes a habit, but until *you* become 'focusing' itself. This is not easy, and it takes time to learn. We are all victims of time: our busy lives require much of us, and our Minds seem to be everywhere. But this is not a great problem if you are 'focused' properly.

"Do this today: *Relax totally* and *focus completely*. If this is done properly you will find your whole body is in a state of relaxed awareness and even 'time' itself will seem to be in slow motion. When that happens it will be impossible for you to have an agitated mind.

"Also, try to observe yourself sometime when you are not in a state of relaxed awareness. You will be surprised at how tense your body is: you may notice your jaw is tightly clenched and your arms and hands are tense. Learning to be in a state of ease will be of immense benefit to you. Value it. After all, it may help you to live longer. Also, from now on, try to *become* what you need to be. You have learned to bring your 'focusing' *up to* and *inside* yourself. Don't think *outside* yourself, think *inside* yourself.

"Let me tell you about the famous Zen Master Bankei. He was asked by a monk to explain something. 'When I go to sleep,' said the monk, 'I sometimes dream. Why do I dream?' The Master replied, 'If you are really in a deep sleep, you will not have dreams. Dreams do not occur when you sleep deeply.'

"Whether this is right or not in the light of present-day understanding of dreams I do not know, but I do know that when you meditate deeply and properly, your Mind will not wander, your Mind will not dream. If you are not 'doing it properly' your Mind *will* wander and at that moment meditation ceases. Many times you will feel exasperated because your Mind *will* wander, but please do not become distressed. Your Mind after all is very much like a puppy that has to be trained, by constant repetition. At first you will be doing well if you meditate properly for a few minutes only. Bit by bit you will add to that, from two minutes to three, then five, seven, ten and twenty, and more still. Then you will find that it is happening almost without you directing it. But you should practise every day. Doing it Monday, then forgetting Tuesday or Wednesday is not really good. Snatch time, steal time—a moment here, a moment there—but do it every day.

"When I first spoke with you seven days ago I suggested that you do your practice in a casual manner, whilst sitting, or standing, and I had a reason for that. But now I want you to practise in a more structured way. Each day, find some time to be alone. Seat yourself in a position that you can maintain but do *not* slouch. Try not to lean your back against support: preferably sit straight. Try to make your period of 'sitting' a routine, even if only for a few minutes at first. Later you can build on this and aim for longer periods. It is better not to be too cold, or too hot, or to try to 'sit' after a large meal.

"Let me tell you what I do. I have a busy life but I always ensure that I 'sit' for at least a half hour each day. I sit on the floor, but even after many years I find sitting in lotus difficult, so I use the kneeling position. This is especially good when hips and knee joints can cause pain. I place a cushion under my shins and also one under my backside—two cushions if necessary. This is not uncommon, even amongst Zen practitioners. If you are young, a daily period of agony, twisting your legs to do what they may not want to do, might not be wasted effort, but if you are older, or very old, it is a matter of being sensible. After all, it is your *Mind* that is being trained, not your legs.

"Please 'sit' as tall as you can, and make sure your backbone is straight and firm. The rest of you must be relaxed, especially your belly. It is not necessary to hold your hands in the classic Zen position: just hold one with the other—either one, it doesn't matter. There are some who advocate strict observance of all traditional postures and positions, but you are not monks and 'sitting' formally is of no consequence. No sin is committed if you do not observe these traditions.

"In a traditional temple the situation is quite different. It is much better if everyone does not do 'their own thing.' But for you, 'sit' straight, hold your chin in and keep your mouth closed. Your eyes must be open. Lower them as though you were looking about three feet in front of you. Do not lower your head. Hold your neck straight and although your chin is pulled in, you should not arch your neck. Straight and firm, yet relaxed and alert. Then relax your focus. Things might appear a little blurred. It is better if nothing takes your attention away from your meditation.

"Very softly, say 'one' to yourself. Imagine you are a hollow column and that the sound of 'one' sinks slowly into your chest, then into your belly. Just as fine sand would sink to the bottom of a column of water, imagine 'one' is 'settling' down inside you. Every time you breathe out, say 'one' and, as you breathe in, imagine your thoughts are sinking down inside you. Your Mind should *not* be outside yourself, as though you were 'looking' at it happen: go *inside* yourself and become 'one.' You must sink down inside yourself. Let your *Mind* and your *awareness* become 'one.'

"My own teacher insisted on the importance of breath control. His instruction was that the outgoing breath should be slow and even and never forced, and that the incoming breath should happen naturally. After a few months of practice your breathing rate should be four or five breaths a minute, sometimes even less. When this happens, one's mind-state will also become slow and even.

"There are those who describe a place, a little below and a little behind your navel area, where there is a special area of consciousness. It is often referred to as the *tanden* or *tanzien*. In Japan this vital area is sometimes referred to as the *hara*. It is a mistake to try to locate a special feeling there and much valuable time can be wasted searching for such things. Your body is full of such places where one can locate vague responses. Many students delude themselves into thinking such physiological responses are a measure of their success. Do not confuse yourself with such ideas. What I have been telling you is quite different. All I want you to do is keep your body relaxed, especially your belly, and make it your 'centre.' When I tell you to think of 'three,' or 'two,' or 'one,' or whatever, don't carry it in your head, carry it in your belly. Imagine that 'one' is *within* you.

"Also, please do not search for the so-called 'third eye.' Do not practise esoteric exercises that involve feelings in the crown of your head, or elsewhere. If you are destined to be a part of those traditions, wait until a genuine teacher comes your way. Remember, 'when the student is ready the teacher appears.' I do not teach those things as they are not of my tradition.

"What I want you to do today is this: fill your belly with 'one' and carry it with you everywhere. Imagine 'one' feels very heavy, then let the feeling change until it becomes lighter and lighter until it is scarcely there at all. Suddenly, quite suddenly, you may find it is no longer there at all and all you are left with is a feeling of subtle awareness. Some call this feeling the 'void.' It is not a feeling of emptiness but rather one of *no-thing-ness*, quite different from a feeling of *nothing*. You might keep this sense of vital awareness for only a few seconds before it goes. It seems that almost always this feeling is interrupted. It is as though your Mind is uncomfortable without the myriad of things that it usually has to cope with. What does interrupt you is usually very trivial. It is as though you will contrive any way at all to interrupt your meditation. You must be patient with yourself and do *not* become irritated. You must remember that up until now you have always filled your lives with things—always there is talk, or music, or thoughts of desire, or even simple thoughts about how you will plan your daily activities. This has been a part of your daily habits. But meditation is a place where you must go, and a state you must experience, without these things.

"Life must go on and of course you will not, or cannot, leave the ordinary world. As Master Rinzai said: 'He stands in the midst of a busy throng yet never leaves his original self.' The 'creative void' is where you can be 'at one' with your original self. Of course you have always been 'one' but your life in the everyday world has split you in two. Meditation training makes you realize your 'oneness' again. But it won't happen on its own—it takes training. Success *will* come through subtle awareness, not aimless wandering. My own teacher led me to understand that it takes an 'act of will' to search for 'oneness,' but it takes an 'act of submission' to become it. When the 'act of will' and the 'act of submission' are in perfect balance, and merge to become 'one,' at that moment you are part of the '*one that is within you and all about you.*'

"This is the meditation experience. When you have reached this point, even for a brief moment, you have achieved another dimension. *You are part of an under-standing that goes beyond understanding.*

"Be warned though: it is not a matter for pride, or even pleasure, and if those feelings do intrude, everything of value, except the memory of it, vanishes. As all who have been there know to their sadness, this loss of 'unity' strikes more deeply than any other loss that we as human beings can experience.

"We can all slip backwards, and most of us do. We are a part of life and often 'living' is difficult. But 'actions have consequences' and 'the bills must be paid.' Ordinary life is 'fetching the wood and carrying the water' and it cannot be otherwise, but you have the choice of which way you do it. You won't always bring honor upon yourself, in the way you do the things of life, but when you do 'slip backwards' what do you do? You go back to 'one' again: 'one'... 'one'... 'one.'

"Now please go to your practice. Tomorrow we say our farewells."

The Farewell

Our seven-day period with the Master had concluded. None of us knew whether this short time with him would touch our lives only lightly, or whether it would have a much longer-lasting effect. At the conclusion of our last meditation period, he had seen each of us separately and had questioned us closely, but had asked us not to discuss this. He had said that he too would be interested to know whether or not such a short exposure to meditation would have any lasting effect. He also wondered whether future occasions, similar to ours, would be justified. He regretted the fact that in this Dharma-ending age, so few people were prepared to listen to the voice 'within and all about.' He said:

"You have taken seven steps towards your original self. Of course, in such a short time, it doesn't seem possible to teach you that which has taken others many lifetimes to learn. On the other hand, emancipation *can* come in the flash of an instant. Here is my last message to you:

"Do not despair for the years that have passed... use whatever time you have left without needlessly wasting

it. Life is like a busy street: mind that you do not care-
lessly bump into those who share your way, nor should
you waste time prolonging useless conversations. Do not
push your message onto others, but do not ignore people
who seem less developed or less fortunate than you. Be
wise with your help and be compassionate in your
actions.

"Each day, Zennists say their vows. If you practise your
meditation properly and always keep the feeling of self-
doubt close to you, vows will not be necessary: you will *live*
the vows, and the essence of them will not only be an
obligation but a desire.

"I cannot make you meditate: no one can give you that
experience second-hand. You will either do it or you won't.
Always remember that the knowledge you seek is already
within you and all about you. When it is put to use in the
everyday world, for profit or gain, it is only 'ordinary
knowledge.' However, when that knowledge becomes part
of 'living wisdom', it is also of the ordinary world, but it
then has no limits and dwells everywhere. It becomes
'wisdom in action.' If meditation has one reward that is in
some way measurable, it is the surprise you will feel in not
having 'understood' it all before.

"My own Master told me: 'You are "one" ... and "one" is
you ... there is no distinction between the two. So long as
there is any distinction, Zazen (meditation) is the way to
make them "one." When that happens you will live in
"one" from morning 'til night.' I hope you will experience
this. If or when you do you will wonder where you have
been all your life.

"Soon you will go back into the outside world and I
would like you to take with you my own Master's message
to me. He said:

'With progress in your Zazen you should, as a matter of course, begin to feel gratitude. Without gratitude, meditation is not enough. Eventually, when you share your gratitude with other people, it has no end.'

"There is little more I can say to you and it is important that I do not try. From now, and for the rest of your lives, all the teachings of all the Masters can be summed up in one word: 'one.' But that word can mean nothing to you, or everything. Keep listening to their teaching. You must also keep asking yourselves: 'Am I doing it properly?' That is important. Nothing else remains for me to say except to hope that one day you *will* realize your *oneness*."

With the Master's farewell, each of us left the Temple to return to our separate lives. What we had experienced was, as the Master put it, a mere glimpse of what might be possible, should our aspirations be firm enough. He reminded us again: "You will either do it, or you won't."

MYSELF, OTHER-SELF, ONESELF

Introduction

The earlier meditation teaching, the Pure Wind, which took the form of a one-week "workshop" or "retreat," was circulated privately for some years and on its journey developed a life different from that intended. As with all such teachings, many who undertook the study found that it resulted in more questions than answers. This was not entirely unexpected, but what was not emphasized was that the answers sought would have come from an appeal directed "inwards" rather than "outwards."

Myself, Other-self, Oneself is a teaching developed in response to our insistence on asking questions and, like the earlier teaching, it is in workshop form. Although this is a written teaching it must be stressed that it should not be read continuously from beginning to end. Each day should be taken as a separate teaching and a separate practice. In this modern age there is a tendency to seek "short cuts," but in this case these are to no avail because the act of meditation cannot be hurried. Meditation must work *on you*—not *you on it.*

It should also be stressed that although the Master who taught me belonged to the Zen tradition he was insistent that this should not cause concern for followers of other traditions, for the perceived barriers that exist between different religions are often illusory. There are many "Ways" and throughout history many true teachings have come from Masters outside the tradition of Dharma training.

On one occasion the Master was asked who had made the major contribution to religious understanding in Japan. I wondered who he would name. "Why, Shinran Shonin of course," he replied. This response caused some surprise because Shinran was a renowned Master of the Pure Land, a sect which, although its origins are believed to go back to the vows of Amida Buddha, was nonetheless different from the Zen tradition. This simple statement released us from the bondage of pride, a fault most of us possessed in full measure.

The Master continually insisted that there are countless well-trodden paths to freedom and emancipation. For some, the path demands enormous effort, but for those who follow a different path, the richness of their reward can come almost like a miracle, outside or beyond personal effort. In Japan, these two ways are known as *jiriki* and *tariki*, which mean 'self power' and 'other power,' or 'self help' and 'other help,' although followers of each can be surprised at the way those paths eventually merge. In the final analysis, if the path to personal enlightenment is to be truthfully followed and the goal of emancipation reached, both ways must lose their identity and become One Way.

When we approach this point in our journey we will be nearing release from the bondage of our conceit and the wastefulness of our persistent questions. But as long as questions persist we must find a way to be set free, because it is only when the need for answers is transcended that our journey becomes less arduous. But how, you may ask? The Pure Wind teaching pointed out one Way, and this teaching points out another: the destination, however, is the same.

Those who have experienced even an intimation of what may lie beyond "the cloud barrier," or felt the briefest movement of the "Pure Wind," will know in the depths of their being that the reality for which we are constantly searching is within us and all about us. For most of us, however, the Way is often cloudy and the paths seem too many and we become fearful of losing our way. But in the midst of fear, confusion, and even desperation, it is still held to be true that when "the student is ready, the teacher appears," pointing the way along the Living Road.

Although the earlier teaching, *The Pure Wind*, was sent to the Master for his comments, this present offering was incomplete at the time of his departure from this life. The author accepts any errors as his own and can only hope that this teaching might have gained the Master's approval.

Meeting
the
Master

It was the day prior to the commencement of the "retreat" and the small group who were to participate gathered together to meet the Master.

We were all "lay" people, mostly from the West. Some of us had come from other countries especially to take part in the retreat, and would return after it was completed. Others lived in Japan permanently while others had spent short periods of time there, teaching or studying. All of us, however, had previously undertaken study with the Master and had attended the Temple as often as our individual circumstances allowed: sometimes a few hours each day, or perhaps only once or twice weekly.

But at certain times during the year we were expected to spend a more concentrated period at the Temple to participate in a "retreat" or "workshop" which coincided with a special time in the Buddhist calendar. That most of us were not Buddhists, in the usual sense, was quite unimportant to the Master. What we were undertaking transcended religious differences and at no time was there even the slightest indication of any intention to "convert" us.

Although most had met before, some of us did not know all of the other participants' names, nor from where they had come. What was strange to many of us from the West was that no names were taken on the day we met, neither were there personal introductions, roll calls or fees. Generally we met at the Temple door and perhaps chatted until we were invited inside, but mostly we met and left in silence. We were told that we should not spend time in idle talk, especially after meditation, but to "carry the fruits of meditation" with us for as long as possible.

On the day of our arrival the Master was working in the garden. There was a reason for meeting there because nothing he did was without purpose. After greeting us he said:

"When I work in my garden I know I must dig deep if I wish to sweeten the soil. I must go down deep to reach the richer nutrients that are buried there. In meditation, you must dig deep too; it is much the same as tending a garden. But remember when you go to your garden to work, although it is *you* who prepares the soil and it is *you* who puts the plants in the ground and it is *you* who gives them water and nourishment and pulls out the weeds, it is *not* you who makes the plants grow. Something apart from you makes them grow. *You* care for them but you cannot make them grow. It is in their *nature* to grow—they grow of themselves. When they don't grow properly there is always a reason: diseases, lack of nutrients, or a continuing struggle with the stronger weeds.

"In meditation there are weeds with which we must compete. Mostly they are too strong for us, but we rarely admit it. One of these is the weed of excuses. We are always busy—so much goes on in our lives we often don't have the time to think clearly, let alone get our lives in some order. Is this one of the reasons why you are here? For peace and quiet? That is not why you are here. You are here to do your gardening—to pull out the weeds that are poisoning your 'mind-soil' and which impede your natural growth. This week we shall get rid of the weeds. I have an ancient remedy. We shall use poison to fight poison.

"Some of you have come from places far away to attend our 'workshop.' You have come on a journey to begin another journey. Meditation is a journey and it is also a voyage of discovery. Many times you will think you have reached your destination only to find you are just beginning. Also, sometimes just when you think the direction you are taking is right, it is as likely to be wrong and you have lost your way. What is even more difficult is that you must travel a lot of the way on your own because each of us must take different paths. We may travel with somebody else part of the way, but finally each of us must find our own way to the journey's end.

"So where *are* we going if we can't know our destination until we have arrived, and we are not sure which paths to follow? To take such a journey will need great faith. Where do we find this faith that will carry us along the way?

"*True faith* comes of itself. What do I mean by 'it comes of itself'? I cannot tell you that either... It just does. One day you will suddenly realize that you not only *have* faith, you *are* faith. Ask yourselves why you are here today, in this Temple. Is it *faith* that brought you here, or *hope*?

"You have already begun your journey. Tomorrow we shall continue on our way."

The First Day

We met together early on the first morning of our meditation retreat. The Master spoke to us briefly:

"Recently I was asked by a Western visitor whether or not meditation is nothing more than developing a state of mind that really does little other than 'make one feel good.' The same person also thought that a daily period of active thinking was much more important and that if we followed Socrates' dictum 'know thyself' we would be sure to find inner peace.

"But what is 'knowing oneself'? If we knew the answer to that perhaps we would find inner peace.

"We use a lot of ifs in our daily lives: 'if only we were not so busy'; 'if only we had more time'; if this, or if that... Always the 'if' is there. If we are truthful we use too many excuses as to why we do not do things and these excuses usually begin with 'if.' But what do we mean by 'if'? Today we might find out.

"You are all experienced in meditation but each day I will remind you of some important details we tend to forget. It is often the case that the more experienced we *think* we are, the more time we waste. You might be surprised at how much meditation time is not used properly.

"Go to your places and sit down as you have been shown. You must position yourselves comfortably because excessive discomfort will interfere with what you have to do. But do not sit too comfortably or you will be tempted to doze. Keep your back straight, your chin held in, and your neck a little arched, but not so that you experience pain. After you are seated you must start your Mind exercises as you have been shown. I will repeat what you must do.

"Firstly, look at something in front of you, but look at it in slow-motion, because you *must slow down your mind processes*. I want you to lower your gaze and look at the floor a few feet in front of you. You will find some small area on which you can focus your eyes. Look slowly and softly, as if your eyes and whatever you look at were fully merging. I have told you before that mostly we do not see things in absolute focus. Once our senses have recognized and filed away a piece of information, we tend to relax our focus. But I want you to really, *really* focus and *keep* that focus for more than just a brief moment. You will remember that proper focusing should not be strained, instead it should be soft and relaxed, as though it was happening in slow-motion. *Focusing is mind training.*

"At this point your attention or awareness will be *outside* yourself because you *are* focusing on something that *is* outside yourself. Then when you are really relaxed and 'in focus' I want you to half close your eyes, at which point you will lose your eye focus. You must then shift your concentration to a point just above your eyes, between your eyebrows. This is not difficult to do but if you wish you can practise it a few times to become familiar with the feeling.

It is very simple: all you are doing is shifting your 'presence of mind,' your 'awareness' or your 'focusing,' from *outside* to *inside*. Once mastered it is quite easy. Then let this relaxed awareness sink down very slowly inside yourself. Imagine that your body is a hollow column and that your thoughts and feelings are to fill every part of it. You can also practise this a few times by bringing your awareness back up between your eyebrows, then letting it sink down again. Then very slowly and softly say 'if'... but say it silently, to yourself, 'if'... 'if'... 'if'... 'if'... At first there will the temptation to add something else to the word: '*If* only I had *money*'... or '*free time*'... or whatever. You should by now be quite competent at detecting the wanderings of your mind and so you will avoid your mental meanderings.

"Next, I want you to say '*if*' with a slightly rising inflexion, as though you were beginning to ask a question: 'if?' 'if?' 'if?' With a little practice you will learn to change the emphasis of the word.

"Just say if? and let it *go deep* inside you... Let it slowly sink under the usual babble that occupies our minds. As you breathe in, say 'if?' and as you breathe out say 'if?' '*If*' *will fill up your whole mind and body until there seems to be not one empty space.*

"It is possible that you might experience a slight feeling of anxiety... of being 'on edge.' This is to be expected because you are asking something, but you are not sure why, and this will cause uncertainty. This tension or uncertainty is not a bad thing, but do not try to make it happen—it is not important. I have told you before that you must have *trust*... and you must have *faith*. Both are important. Trust is something you can decide upon, but faith must grow, and it will grow of itself.

"Just ask 'if?' 'if?' 'if?'" You are asking a question for which there is no answer: 'if?' Go to your places... Go to your meditation... *Become* your meditation and remain with it until you are told to stop. I shall see you again tomorrow."

The Second Day

We met early on our second day together, and prior to going to the Meditation Hall the Master addressed us:

"Our lives revolve around questions. One loses count of the number we ask just to cope with everyday living. Think of the thousands of times we ask 'why?' Why are you doing this or that? Why do you say the things you do? Why are you late? Why did you come so early? The 'whys' go on and on, endlessly. A child asks a lot more 'whys' than we do but that is to be expected: everything is new to a child and they ask 'why?' as part of the process of learning. When we grow up we know a lot of the answers already and so we don't ask as many questions, but despite this, deep down inside us there is always a 'why' which is never answered and which causes us to have feelings of unease and even anxiety. I call this the 'ever-present *why*.' This is the biggest 'why' anyone can ask.

"It is a very common thing for children to feel frightened of the dark because it is full of things unseen and unknown. When they grow up life is still full of things unknown, and this uncertainty often brings a sense of helplessness and futility. This is because deep within us is the feeling that no matter how well we cope with life, or how well we plan our strategies for successful living, in the long run it all amounts to nothing. Life is never totally satisfying because nothing is certain, except of course our departure from it.

"We are never really cut off from suffering. We may bury our uncertainties and our anxieties deep inside us and cover them over with layers of activities and possessions, but deep down we still know it is an exercise in futility.

"An early Buddhist teaching states that for the unenlightened person, life is suffering and that all suffering is caused by desire. We are also taught that this can be transcended. It could be said that suffering, and a wish to escape from it or rise above it, is the very basis of the religious instinct. Many people pray to their gods in the hope that they will be protected from the pain of life. Others hope that at the end of life they will be transported to a better life where no one dies. But will this be so?

"If we really want to be free of the pain of life and also achieve religious fulfillment, we must transcend not only our desire to escape from pain but even the desire for fulfillment. Which brings us to our task for today.

"Today I want you to ask the question 'why?' Just 'why?' Nothing else. It seems easy, but you will realize it is not so. I want you to bring to that word *all the presence of your mind. Nothing* else should intrude on your thoughts.

"Now please listen carefully. Go to your meditation places. Straighten your back, slightly arch your neck and pull your chin in. Do your slow-motion soft-focusing and then shift your presence of mind to a spot between your eyebrows. Say 'why?' to yourself, slowly and softly, over and over, then let the word sink down and fill up all the corners of your body. Repeat the process. Shift your awareness back up to your head then let it sink back down again. Say 'why' very softly to yourself, then even more softly...until it disappears. When it reappears, or when your mind wanders, repeat the process. While you are concentrating on saying 'why' very little else will enter your mind. *But* as you lose your attentiveness a myriad of vague thoughts will intrude and in a flash your 'why' has gone and your mind is wandering. The more experienced you become the sooner you will notice that your attention has wandered. It is important though that you do not suppress those thoughts that are intruding—just observe them, and let them fade away.

"The question we should ask ourselves is this: If *we* are not consciously putting anything into our minds, except the word 'why,' where do the other thoughts come from?

"We read a lot about the 'conscious,' the 'subconscious' and the 'unconscious,' but for the purpose of our meditation exercise I do not want to use those terms, whatever they may mean. Instead let us say that the thoughts we construct or the questions we ask all come from the MYSELF part of me, whilst the other seemingly unbidden thoughts come from the OTHER-SELF part of me. Most of the time our MYSELF mind is getting on with the business of life, yet other thoughts seem to float up, seemingly from nowhere, then sink out of sight again.

"For the greater part of our lives we work with bits and pieces of information that are readily available to us, yet there is a whole lot more vital knowledge which seems to be largely unavailable. It is as though it is locked away, or largely unused, only occasionally breaking the surface of the MYSELF mind.

"The Mind is a mysterious mechanism: it houses many things, some of which we do not seem to have learned, but which must have been born in us, already formed. This information floats up into the MYSELF mind then, when it is not required, it sinks away 'out of mind.' Sometimes it seems to bypass the awareness of the MYSELF mind and is not even registered.

"The OTHER-SELF part of us is such a huge repository of information it is beyond speculation. But what *is* available in the OTHER-SELF affects our lives in ways we don't even know. The OTHER-SELF is the place where our instincts live, and maybe too, all the ghosts of our unknown or deeply buried past. We can't possibly measure how much is there, deeply hidden, and only occasionally do we sense its presence. Even if we were given the chance to take an inventory of what *was* there, not many would care to do so. But along with everything else to be found in the OTHER-SELF, there are rewards beyond imagination, and it is these we should seek.

"What we are doing this week *will take us beyond* the everyday ordinary mind to levels *deeper* than we thought possible. This week we must learn to go beyond the limited knowledge of the MYSELF to seek the wisdom of the OTHER-SELF.

"Now please go and ask the question 'why?,' and when you have finished here today still try to keep that thought inside you. Just 'why?' ... Do not look for answers. 'Why?' 'Why?' 'Why?' Your OTHER-SELF is deep within you. You *must* go deep into your inner, OTHER-SELF and ask 'why?' I will see you again tomorrow."

The Third Day

"This week you are asking many questions, but I must remind you not to look for, or even hope for, an answer. If one does come it is sure to be in a way you do not expect. To look for an answer, or to predict what it might be, is a mistake—let everything happen of its own accord.

"When we were children many of our questions began with 'what?': 'What is this?'; 'What is that?' We also used to ask 'who?': 'Who is that person?'; 'Who are you?' When we ask 'who' we usually want some identification— a name to fit a face. But the 'who' question is perhaps not as important as the 'what' question. For example, we know *who* we are but we do not always know *what* sort of person we are. We think we know, but we can never *really* be sure.

"On the surface we are one person but we have been assembled from many different pieces. For example: each one of us had two parents; they had four; those four had eight parents; and they had sixteen. Going back only twenty generations involves us with over one million forebears. Each one of us here in this room is the outcome of a genetic contest, the result of which has determined our skin and hair color, height, predisposition to certain traits, liability to certain illnesses and a lot more besides. Scientists can do many evaluations these days but they still cannot measure or predict the subtle combinations that determine personality and character.

"To some extent we are victims of a past we have not even known—at least not consciously. It is true that some of our genetic characteristics can be modified by our upbringing, but no matter how carefully we are nurtured there are still some ghostly echoes within us which link us with our past.

"One thing we do know is that this accumulation of nerves, cells, instincts, knowledge and beliefs we call Me does not always live in harmony with itself. These separate parts seem to behave as though they too were in contest, each wanting to be independent yet having to be interdependent. We do know that every part of us follows a pattern of growth and decline, and no one has ever been able to stop that cycle. We are born, we grow to maturity, and then we die. No plant or tree or any form of animal life seems able to bypass death. For all our differences this is one thing we have in common.

"But the chemists tell us that 'nothing is wasted,' and that a basic law of chemistry is that 'all matter strives for a greater stability.' Is it possible that we too are striving for a similar stability and security? And is it because we cannot know this perfection of self, and also, instinctively, we sense our inevitable loss of a personal identity, that we experience anxiety, even dread? Is this why we fill our lives with a myriad of things—to forget how short life is? Is this why some of us run around frantically, trying this or that religion, hoping for a personal 'salvation' through which we might transcend our ordinary mortal limits? Is this why *you* are here this week?

"Whether we know it or not, the *'oneness'* we seek is within and all about us, but *when* we do not *know* it, we are at the mercy of our own inner conflict. Can we avoid this conflict? We are told by all the sages that the *really* enlightened person knows *no* conflict. It is also held to be true that real meditation, proper meditation, can bring us closer to a *'oneness'* that transcends conflict.

"I have spoken about the MYSELF and the OTHER-SELF. The voice of the OTHER-SELF speaks from an entirely different level to that of everyday life. It is the voice of the OTHER-SELF, rising within us, that reminds us we are not yet complete. But we do not usually hear the voice of the OTHER-SELF, because the words are often no more than a murmur, almost lost in the business of everyday living. But because the MYSELF is aware of them, even if only as a vague feeling or premonition, we are left with a feeling of unease. We are like people who awake from a dream, not knowing *who* or *where* they are.

"During this meditation workshop we are trying to transcend the limits of our ordinary thinking so that we can hear the OTHER-SELF more clearly, to finally *know* within ourselves the security of our *'oneness.'*

"Already I have spoken about my garden, and the work that needs to be done. Our meditation practice is like gardening: we are digging the soil deeper so that the roots of our 'Mind-plants' can reach the nutrients which will help them grow in a less stunted way. Those nutrients come from the wisdom of the OTHER-SELF but you have to reach into your depths to find it.

"Today we are asking 'what.' *What* sort of person might I become if my Mind-roots reach those richer nutrients?

Will those nutrients help my worldly cleverness or deepen my wisdom? Will I transcend my limitations? *What* could happen? *What* might happen? *What* will happen?

"'What' is the word you must live with today, but you must do it with all the strength of your being. The MYSELF cannot make the OTHER-SELF answer but you can open your ears and mind and heart to hear the message.

"YOU ask and the OTHER-SELF answers. Do *not* supply the answer yourself—that is futile. When the time is right, the answer will come by itself. Just ask 'what?' This will help you get rid of your mind-weeds.

"Do not be tense, just pay attention. Keep your back straight but keep your insides relaxed. If you become tense, practise your soft-focusing, in slow-motion. But let the focusing take place inside yourself—*inside* not *outside*. As you become more experienced you will begin to notice that there are those whose speech comes from their whole being, while that of others appears to come from some place *outside* themselves. So remember always: *inside*, *not outside*.

"Today I will 'sit' with you and together we will take the word 'what' deep down *inside* us. Say the word softly to yourself, in your mind. It might help if you form your lips as you say the word.

"You will remember that you can place the word wherever you want it to be—behind the forehead, or in the right ear or the left ear. You can place it deep in your chest and you can let it fill your belly, your arms and legs. You can choose where *you* want the word to be because *it is all done in the mind—your mind*.

"Let the word fade away so that it is just a whisper: it is there, inside you still, but scarcely discernible.

"If your mind begins to wander say it *loud* inside you, as though you were calling it out to someone, but then let it fade away into the silence again. Above all, you must be relaxed—*relaxed* but *aware*.

"I shall leave you to your work."

The Fourth Day

The Master reminded us that we were at the midway point of our meditation workshop:

"This is Day Four and there are only three more left after this one. *How* much have we achieved these last few days? *How* is it possible for us to know if we have achieved anything at all? Abstract thoughts are difficult to measure so let us first turn to something practical.

"For some of you the concept of 'going inside oneself' is still difficult and you are not sure if you are doing it properly. *How* can I make it clearer? It is, of course, all in the mind. Going inside oneself is not very different from eating an apple or some other food. You take the word I give you then imagine it going into your mouth. You then chew and swallow the word and it ends up in your belly. It is really very easy, once you have the idea. But you must go further than that: you must relax your whole belly area and imagine the word fills up the whole space.

"In the East the belly area is very important: it is your 'center' and I want you to imagine that is where you will find your OTHER-SELF. Of course the OTHER-SELF is not there but for the purposes of our training it is best for you to place your mind there. If you allow your mind to jump all over the place you will become confused and distracted and that will work against your meditation practice. It is natural that your mind will want to escape from the discipline you impose on it but you mustn't let it.

"I am asking you to do two things which seem contradictory. On the one hand I ask you to discipline your mind, but then I tell you I want you to relax that discipline so that your mind can go into your OTHER-SELF. For some of you this may be difficult, even a little frightening, because there seems to be more safety in staying within the control of your MYSELF. But you must learn to leave your MYSELF if you wish to meditate properly. You must learn to *trust* yourselves.

"It is not always easy to trust ourselves. In our OTHER-SELF repository there are many very complex instincts and these, like many of our feelings, are a source of conflict. So how do we come to terms with them, and how do we learn '*trust*'? We may not be able to do much about our feelings but at least we do have some *choice* in the way we react to them. It may not be the right one, but we still have been able to make that choice. Of course, many of the choices we make are of no great consequence either way, but others are very important and might even be a matter of life or death.

"But what is it that determines our choice? *How* does this happen? It is true to say that there are some actions which are *possible* for us to take yet there are others which we would find *impossible*. For most of us, murder would be impossible. In times of war perhaps we might accept the notion of killing a little more readily, but even then, for many of us, killing would still be very difficult. Why?

Because it *offends* against some feeling, deep within us. Of course it is possible to override these feelings and revert to a more primitive type of behavior, but when this does happen, it is usually at some personal cost and we usually regret it.

"Feelings have a lot to do with our behavior. How often do we say 'I don't *feel* that this is right,' or 'I *feel* this is wrong.' These feelings help us decide what to do. Sometimes our *feelings* are blurred and this makes us confused, but despite this we still have the ability to override or modify our feelings. We can *choose* between alternatives.

"But what determines our choice? Our feelings might come from the OTHER-SELF, but it is our MYSELF that makes the decisions, either good or bad. Our MYSELF mind sorts through all the information available to it and *decides* which way to go.

"In most religious teachings it is believed that right *aspiration* is the beginning of right *action*, and it is in the *rightness* of your aspiration that you find your protection. It goes without saying that if all of us here today *aspire* to a *higher state* of awareness and to a *higher state* of being, we have already begun to achieve it. The fact that the MYSELF aspires to seek the deeper wisdom of the OTHER-SELF is not only the first step towards achieving a deeper dimension of Self, it leads to the path that will take us towards eventual self-liberation. But to do this effectively we must learn *trust* and find *faith*.

"It seems complicated, but it is not. We have *aspiration*, then *action*. With practice we learn *knowledge*. Accumulated knowledge becomes *wisdom* and this leads to the unfolding of *faith* and *trust*. This is the path to enlightenment.

"How does this miracle happen? We must ask 'how?' This brings us back to today's question, today's word: 'how?'

"*How* can we transcend our limited view of life? The aspirations of the MYSELF take us part of the way but the answer we seek must come from somewhere else. You have come part of the way through asking 'ifs' and 'whys' and 'whats.' Now is the time to ask 'how?'

"Before you go to your work there are more questions I must answer. Some of you are experiencing 'strange' feelings during meditation, for example unusual heat in the hands. This is quite normal and is usually an indication that your hands are very relaxed; it will not happen if your body and arms and hands are tense. It is also quite normal for your whole body to feel warm, especially when you are doing your work properly. It is only when your meditation is finished that you feel cold again. Warmth is supposed to indicate a good 'energy' flow, which occurs only when you are relaxed. Also common is a feeling of small shuddering waves, like a shivering sensation, yet you are not cold. Don't worry, that too is natural. I have also known some who have seen brilliant colors and intense light, especially when they close their eyes. If this happens just notice it and return to your question. When you are in a relaxed and hypersensitive state many odd things can happen, but none of them are important and most certainly, you should not try to produce them.

"The only other thing you should be reminded about is to always keep in the back of your mind the 'feeling of doubt,' but this must not become a feeling of anxiety. Remember that meditation is a perfect balance between an 'act of will' and an 'act of submission.' Your MYSELF takes you there—that is an act of will—but your OTHER-SELF will only yield its wisdom through the act of submission. If your *aspiration* is right, you should not fear going into the unknown of the OTHER-SELF. Right *aspiration* is your protection. Now please go. We shall meet again tomorrow."

Where

The Fifth Day

"This is our fifth day and the questions we have been asking should now be deep within us. At this point in our training we should ask *where* have we reached. 'Where' is our word for today.

"I have several reasons for giving you this word as today's *koan*. You already know that a 'koan' is somewhat like a riddle but one with an answer that cannot be arrived at intellectually. My teacher's koan was the word 'one', and he instructed us to take the word deep within us. We wrestled with 'one', wondering what it really meant and why the Master had chosen it. What he really wanted from us was not our understanding of 'one' but of *oneness*. If we asked ourselves what 'one' really meant, eventually we came to realize that as long as we were sure we had the answer we were sure to be excluding other possibilities. When we said that 'one' possessed this or that attribute, or that it meant this but not that, we were actually getting further away from what the Master wanted.

"So what did he want of us? He was asking us to become *oneness* itself—to realize our *oneness*. He knew that our struggling wouldn't produce the right answer, and that only when we had exhausted ourselves and finally submitted, the answer would come of itself. Of course it took a long time to realize what the Master wanted, and the search is not yet finished. Also, as one continues, the more subtle the search becomes.

"At different times during our training our Master would question us closely about our understanding of 'one.' To shake our belief in ourselves he would challenge us in every way possible. He would ask: '*Where* did you get that idea from—out of your head?' Or he would ask: 'With all your cleverness, *where* do you stand now? If you really understand *oneness where* are *you* in relation to it? If *you* are *here* with me, *where* is the *one*? *Where* does the *one* come from? *Where* does it go? *Where*?'

"The Master was endeavoring to stop us from putting things into convenient compartments and to make us realize that every single thing *is* what it is and has its own nature and behaves according to its nature; yet it is still a part of the whole. But he also wanted us to realize much more than that

"Today we ask 'where?' Of course we know *who* we are, and a little of *what* we are, but we now want to know *where* we are going. Most human beings do not want to know the answer to that question and so never ask it: *Not* asking the question avoids the possibility of finding out that they are hopelessly lost.

"There are simple everyday 'wheres' such as '*Where* shall we meet?' or '*Where* are we going?' But the most important 'where' we must ask is also the one that brings us most fear. We know we will die one day. Will we just disappear into thin air, like the smoke from a fire? How often have we heard people saying of someone, '*Where* did he or she die?'

as if the *where* was almost as important as the death itself. *Where* does anyone die?

"Most of us just 'sail through life' without either asking proper questions or getting the real answers. You must 'rock your boat' a little if you really want answers. If you *really* want answers you must ask questions—little questions and big questions. If you only want little answers, you will ask only little questions; but, if you want real answers to the big questions you *must ask them*.

"Always remember, the right answer *will* come to you but *you* must not impose the answer upon yourself: let it rise up within you, from your OTHER-SELF. This is not only my word, but that of everyone who has trod this path. *You* ask the question, but it is *not* really *your* question at all: it too comes from your OTHER-SELF, from exactly the same place that produces the answer.

"At this stage of our training, I must again caution you about becoming confused. Anxiety and tension are a hindrance, whereas strength of purpose and persistence are helpful and necessary. All the Masters have cautioned against becoming lost in anxieties. Be strong, be persistent and look deeply within yourselves: not just under your ribs and skin but deep within you. I have told you how to do this: let your question sink into your belly. Let your belly soften and expand out. Let your belly fill up with today's question. If you become tense or anxious just remember that our slow-motion focusing routine is your safeguard, and when you feel at ease, take up your question once again. Say to yourself: 'The answer is within me.'

"Now, I want to give you some more advice. It is natural for us to want to protect ourselves from the pain that often accompanies meditation, especially when you are doing it properly. Pain or no pain, at the very least you must 'sit' for a half-hour period before you give in. Your legs might object, your back and your mind might object to the wrestling match in which you are engaged, but rise above it. In the early days of your meditation experience I told you to aim for a shorter period of real concentration, but now you have graduated to a higher level and must take your place amongst those who really know how to struggle. If this proves impossible, try the other way: go about your daily business, keep your questions in your mind and put your faith and trust in the OTHER-SELF. Although this way might be easier on your legs and on your minds, you will have to exercise great skill not to become lost in the myriad of things that can distract you.

"There is a saying: 'outside of mind no other thing.' Of course we know many things happen outside our Minds about which we have absolutely no knowledge, but they only become real to us through the actions of our Minds. You have chosen to undertake your search by struggling with your *Mind* and your *whole self*. *You* have chosen to do this, and it is *you* who will determine just how hard you wish to struggle. But remember, *you* do not supply the answers to your deepest questions—at least not with your intellect—because they come from your OTHER-SELF.

"The MYSELF is what we are mostly concerned about in our everyday lives. It is the MYSELF that demands most of our attention. One way to broaden and deepen the MYSELF is to keep asking: '*Who is this "I" of whom I speak?* Where do all my ideas about myself come from?' The great Masters over the ages have all come to the view that the deepest, most profound wisdom is that which still remains after all our conceptual knowledge has been exhausted and discarded. The ideas that come from the MYSELF fall far short of the wisdom of the OTHER-SELF.

"It is *you* who Aspires to become *one* with your deeper self. It is *you* who will take whatever Action is necessary. But the *you* that you hold so dear and think so important is nothing compared with the *you* that is yet to be found. Your OTHER-SELF knows this, and it is through the action of the OTHER-SELF that you seek the fullness of yourself. You may not hear the voice that speaks softly within you, but it speaks to you all the time. It is your MYSELF that is usually too busy, or too self-interested to heed it.

"From *where* do the deepest and most profound questions arise? *Where* do the most profound answers come from? *Where*?

"I have talked to you long enough. Go and do your work."

when

The Sixth Day

The Master began the session reminding us that it was our second-last day:

"This is Day Six and we have little time left to do our work. Meditation *is* work, but it is also something else. What *is* this *something else*? It is much easier to say what meditation is *not*, rather than what it *is*.

"According to the Zen tradition, during meditation the mind/brain is *not* asleep; it is *not* in a state of blissful repose, nor is it in a state of reverie, or enjoying pleasant daydreams. One or all of these may occur but, if the meditator is well-trained, they will not become permanent. In meditation there is always the danger of reaching a stage where one feels that what is happening is beneficial, comfortable and desirable and it would be very easy to become content with that. But that is *not* where one should stay. Even if that stage does mark a creative point in one's development, it would *not* be creative to keep returning there. As I have said before: one must extend oneself outside and beyond what has already been achieved.

"Some who practise meditation will always be frightened of going beyond what they already know. To be really creative in any field or endeavor one must relinquish the known and go into the unknown. I have already told you that you must develop Faith and Trust, but if you still have fears about losing your way, and even becoming sick in your mind, there is a simple technique which you can practise. If, in your meditation work, you inch forward bit by bit each day, you will become quite used to your Mind having freedom. Meditation is 'natural.' It is not like taking drugs or drinking alcohol to become relaxed: that supposed freedom is merely surrendering to the effect of a chemical. When one meditates one is not stupefying the brain or confusing its activity with chemicals, but rather, allowing it to expand and become enriched.

"Now to work. There is an old saying that 'work is good for us,' and this week I have given you a lot of work to stimulate the flow of thoughts between the MYSELF and the OTHER-SELF. You must never 'lock up' your thoughts but rather, give them something to do.

"When you meditate and open up yourself to the deeper levels of your being, you gain access to profound truths which are difficult to express in words. This wisdom *has* been there all the time but it is like a pool of water where what lies beneath the surface cannot be seen if the surface is agitated, or if the waters themselves are clouded with refuse. Why is it that we do not spend more of our short lives looking under the surface of our selves? There should always be some time in your lives to do this—but *when*? We use 'when' a lot in our daily lives: '*When* are you going to do this?' or '*When* will you have time?' and so on. But let me assure you that we have not really explored *when* anywhere near as much as we should.

"There is another 'when,' not so accurately measured and which intrudes into our lives only vaguely and occasionally. It is the 'when' that tells the time of the biological clock which measures our whole life span. This clock begins *when* we are born and ceases *when* we die. We avoid reading the time of this clock because it fills us with alarm and panic. We do not want to heed it but we cannot ignore the fact that it is there. The MYSELF part of us tries very hard to do this, as we fill up our lives in every conceivable way; but deep within us the OTHER-SELF knows that this is precisely the clock we must heed, measuring as it does, not only our body-time but the disturbing realities of life. It is *this* clock which reminds us of the value of *when*.

"You must take 'when' into yourselves today. *When* you sit, let 'when' fill you up. Think of every sort of 'when,' including those concerned with the trivial things of life. Eventually you will exhaust them and discover that you have been wasting your time. When that happens, you can ask yourself the important 'when.'

"There is a way of asking which will take you very deep within yourself, and will challenge your very being. Find that 'when.' Go to that 'when.' Ask that 'when.' You will find the answer to that 'when' at the very moment you become *one* with your OTHER-SELF.

"When? When? When?

"Your clock is ticking away. Go now and look at the time."

how

The Seventh Day

It was the seventh and final day at the Temple, and our meditation session would not finish until late at night. Before we entered the Meditation Hall for the last time the Master spoke to us:

"You have worked hard this week but I fear that some of you are already taking comfort in your progress. Let me warn you that even after you have taken the 'great leap' outside yourselves to become *one* with the OTHER-SELF, there is always the possibility—mostly it is a probability—of sliding back into old habits. How do you prevent this? It is quite easy—just avoid the bad old ways. When you see danger approaching, step aside and move on, straight ahead. It is true that sometimes danger cannot be avoided, but you still have 'choice.' There is a saying: 'you cannot always have control over what happens to you, but you can control how you react to it.' We all know how quickly our thoughts can gallop out of control. It takes only one flash of thought to become embroiled in a lot of 'mind-madness,' but if you have properly understood what we are doing here this week you will have learned how to apprehend your thoughts before you are at their mercy.

"If? Why? What? How? Where? When? You have confronted all of these so far, and the word you will take to your meditation today is 'now.'

"I shall try and explain what we have been doing this week. All the words I have given you are common everyday words, and no day passes without us using them many times. But in our day-to-day lives they are mostly used in MYSELF situations and, although they may have relative importance in this regard, their use is still limited. This week we have attempted to change that way of thinking. By taking seven simple words, but using them in a totally different way, it is possible to view them quite differently, with surprising results.

"When we began this week I was speaking of gardening and the ever-constant job of removing weeds so that healthy plants can grow. I also said that we need to remove the weeds from our Minds for the right thoughts to grow. Thoughts of desire, anger, envy, greed and hate are not only mind-weeds, they are poisons and can cause 'Mind-madness.' The 'cure' is also a poison and it too must be discarded after it has effected its cure. To take medicine after it is no longer needed can itself cause illness.

"The weeds I speak of all grow in your MYSELF Mind and they have been the cause of your separation from the OTHER-SELF, but when your MYSELF and OTHER-SELF are again *one*, the cure is almost complete. But Mind-weeds are very stubborn and it is only by ridding yourself of them that you will 'open up' your MYSELF to the deeper wisdom of the OTHER-SELF. How does this happen?

"In the meditation state—if it is done properly—chemical and physical changes take place whereby the normal rigidity of the MYSELF becomes softened and the edges of awareness expand beyond their usual limits. When this happens the MYSELF becomes enriched with the higher wisdom of the OTHER-SELF. It is then that our inner potentialities can become reality. But this takes practice. It can happen on its own sometimes but because this is very rare the Masters of old devised and developed techniques to help their students experience the transition.

"I have used the expression 'soft-focusing' many times. There is only one proper way of 'viewing' for an object to be *in focus*. The object of your attention is either *in* focus or *out* of focus. In our everyday living, being *in* or *out* of focus is not really important. Our brain and our past experiences 'fill in' a lot and we don't need to be properly focused. In the early days of our training I asked you to concentrate your attention on something within your vision. Then, when you had learned to do this, I asked you to take that same concentrated awareness deep inside yourself where the focusing was no longer done with your eyes but with your 'Mind's eye.' But even this focusing can be 'in' or 'out.' The ancient Masters knew this, as we have said, and they warned that with 'a tenth of an inch's difference Heaven and Earth were set apart.'

"It is not easy to give you a proper understanding of inner focusing—it can only really be experienced, not explained. But all this week you have been doing exercises to help you become more aware of your inner focusing, to prepare you for the next step, which is the merging of the MYSELF and the OTHER-SELF. These two selves are not separate of course, but because most people spend the greater part of their awareness being concerned only with the MYSELF, the OTHER-SELF, as I call it, has almost disappeared. It is like looking at the flowers blooming on a tree, thinking they are the most important parts, ignoring the trunk, the branches, leaves and roots. With our question words we have been attempting to break down that duality so that once again we may experience everything as *one*.

"My own Master, by using the koan 'one,' encouraged those who studied with him to reach a subliminal understanding of the word 'now,' and today I want *you* to experience that.

"Let us examine the word 'now.' What does it mean? The MYSELF 'now' is the one we mostly use, but the ONESELF 'now' is much different: this 'now' means the moment of present time which has neither beginning nor ending: a state of being, a state of awareness, which is the *now-ness* of the *one-ness* of life itself... But to comprehend it is quite beyond human effort or calculation.

"You *cannot* make this 'now' happen—*it will come as a gift*. When the intellect of the MYSELF merges with the wisdom of the OTHER-SELF, and the act of *will* and the act of *submission* come to a point of perfect balance, then and only then might we know the *now-ness* of *one-ness*. At that point there will be no more MYSELF, no more OTHER-SELF, only the ONESELF. *Now is one: One is now.* 'Now' is your word for today: 'Now'... 'Now'... 'Now.'

"*Now* I will leave you to your work... Tomorrow we say our farewells."

The Farewell

It was early the following day that we met together for our 'farewells.' Most of us would never meet again and for some this was the last occasion they would meet with the Master. He spoke to us for the last time:

"It is time for us to go our various ways but I want to speak with you once more before we say our farewells. I am grateful that you have journeyed here to my temple to take part in this workshop and it is my fervent hope that you will have received benefit even though the experience may have been different from your expectations.

"'Workshop' is a strange modern word. 'Work' is what someone does to earn a living or perform some task. So what is a workshop? Our 'shop' here, where we have been working, really has nothing to sell and nothing to buy. The things you have been seeking are yours anyway and they have been within your grasp all the time. I certainly have nothing that I could rightfully sell and you cannot buy it anyway.

"It is wrong either to buy or sell the fruits of the ONE-SELF. The MYSELF, in everyday life, is always concerned with buying or selling, but the ONESELF cannot sell anything. It is the MYSELF that buys and sells, not the ONESELF. This is not to say that in the modern world it is not right to sell the fruits of one's talents. In a perfect world this would not happen, but our world is not perfect and sadly, most things are sold for the highest possible price.

"Even some religious teachers sell their wares. In this day and age, which is full of sadness and hopelessness, there are always some who have a false message to sell, often to those who are so desperate they must pay the price, however high. Even meditation is sold.

"There is only one price to pay for meditation and that is sincerity.

"In this workshop of ours I have purposely avoided talking about particular religious traditions. According to my tradition, this present period in world history is known as the 'Dharma-ending Age': the period when truth and goodness have become lost to the world. Sadly, just when there is the greatest need for it, religion has not earned for itself great respect. We have many people who pretend to be religious but who will fight to the death for their religions. We have Moslems fighting Moslems, Christians fighting Christians, Buddhists fighting Buddhists; no religion is excluded from this sin and it is all done in the name of some god. What sort of god is that? We are all different: some say 'God'; some say 'Buddha'; others use another name.

"I have read many holy writings. My long period of Zen study has not destroyed for me the holiness of the teachings of Christ, nor the deepest truths of the Koran, or of other writings much older still. I have read many Jewish stories and some are surprisingly similar to those enigmatic stories from the Zen tradition. There are many different

Buddhist traditions too and they answer the differing needs of those who *find* them and are *found* by them. How can one say which is first, second, third or last? Any conflict I have ever felt has been caused by the workings of the MYSELF mind, not the OTHER-SELF mind.

"I have no wish to say anyone is wrong, except those who deny the basic truths of their religions through actions of hate, deception or corruption. No person should fight another in the name of their god because if this *is* the Dharma-ending Age, the fact that anyone has heard even the tiniest of whispered truths, no matter where they come from, should bring joy to us all.

"Amongst those of us who have been here this week there is a diversity of religious commitment, yet our differences have been submerged in the holiest of searches—the quest for *that* which is *holy* within us. The only religion of importance, the *only* religion of any worth, is that which embodies the desire to be at *one* with the Godhead within us and all about us.

"It is not the *name* of the religion that matters: it is *religion* itself. What is religion? It is not to 'know thyself,' as the wise man said: it is to *find* and *be found*. What do I mean by that? It means that although you make the necessary effort to *find* the door which leads to emancipation, *you* yourself cannot open it. No matter how hard you try, how determined you might be, it will only be opened from the other side. When it does open, as it certainly will when the time is right, it is then that you will *be found*. That is what is meant by *to find* and *be found*.

"Let me finish by telling you a story:

"I recall, when I was younger, seeing a very famous set of Chinese ink paintings which had the title *The Ox Herding Pictures*. They portrayed the search of someone who had embarked on a similar journey to the one we have undertaken: the Search we all have to undertake if we wish to find ourselves.

"In the first picture one sees the man looking for the ox. He cannot see the ox but he knows it is to be found somewhere close by. Then he glimpses the ox almost hidden in the undergrowth and sets forth on a chase. He catches the ox and begins the task of taming it. The ox, of course, resists being caught and tamed because it enjoys its life of freedom. But with stubborn determination, bit by bit, the ox is being tamed. The ox herder is then shown riding on the ox's back but still controlling it with rope and stick.

"The next picture shows that the ox has been fully tamed and the ox herder is shown riding it, even facing the wrong way, while playing his flute. The following picture shows that both the ox and the ox herder are missing: both have gained their freedom. The last picture shows the ox herder wandering in the village giving help where and when it is needed. The ox has regained its freedom and is shown wandering the fields enjoying the succulent grasses. It no longer needs the discipline of rope and stick. But the freedom which both the ox and ox herder now enjoy is different from that which they knew before.

"I have read many commentaries on those pictures. Some people think that the ox herder is the MYSELF and that the ox is the OTHER-SELF, but it is actually the other way round. *You*, your MYSELF, is the ox and the ox herder is really your OTHER-SELF. The part of us that needs to be tamed is the MYSELF. I would like you to think about that story.

"This is our last meeting. We all go our own ways now, to the four corners of the Earth. I return to my task, you to yours. Let us be worthy of the vows that have been made on our behalf. It is also important that you do not carry this week with you, except as a guide, because what you have learned here should release you from any bondage, even the one you might think I have imposed upon you. You must always remember that you must never confuse the teacher with the message.

"The Living Road we all search for and hope to tread is within us and all about us. The paths leading to it are numerous and often confusing and we can become lost and afraid, but there are signposts everywhere. All you need do is look for them, find them, then with gratitude, trust and faith, follow where they lead. The rest will happen by itself.

"Seven hundred years ago Daito Kokushi of the Zen tradition followed in the steps of thousands of others who had gone before. In coming to realize the *oneness* 'within and all about,' he expressed his gratitude with the following verse. You have heard it before but I can give you no better farewell.

'Having once penetrated the cloud barrier
The Living Road opens out
North, East, South and West.
In the Evening, resting,
In the Morning, roaming,
Neither Host nor Guest,
At every step the Pure Wind rises.' "

Author's Note:
All royalties from *The Living Road* will go to charity.